2022
ROME

The Restaurant Enthusiast's Discriminating Guide

Andrew Delaplaine

*Andrew Delaplaine is the Food Enthusiast.
When he's not playing tennis,
he dines anonymously
at the Publisher's (considerable) expense.*

James Cubby – Senior Editor

The Restaurant Enthusiast's
Discriminating Guide

<u>Table of Contents</u>

INTRODUCTION

"When in Rome do as the Romans do," and that means enjoying the wonderful food. Visiting Rome may be as much about the food as it is about visiting the museums and historical landmarks. A trip to Rome is certainly not complete without experiencing the food and drink at the many colorful trattorias,

pizzerias, ristorantes and gelaterias. For many years Rome's restaurant scene remained the same and you could stop by a favorite eatery for mounds of pasta but there's been a recent explosion of new restaurants, Panini shops, street-food stalls, bakeries, and cocktail bars run by a new generation of Romans who are adding a new flavor to the ancient city.

Traveling the winding streets of Rome you will find many Italian restaurants in tourist centers. While most restaurants in Rome offer the native cuisine you will also find eateries offering Chinese, Mexican, Indian, and Thai food but beware, the standard is not as high as you will find in other major cities. Once you try the cuisine at the traditional Italian restaurants you probably won't care to try anything else, anyway.

The best way to see Rome is to walk, since the transportation can be a bit unreliable, and you can discover so much more on foot. You'll see a whole world that could never be described in any tour book. You'll be lured by the salespeople, the aroma of a bakery, and possibly find a hidden piazza that seems right out of the 16th century (because it is). You'll wander through neighborhoods filled with families and shops.

There are restaurants everywhere but you should
know a few things before heading out for a meal.
First, realize that the Italians have a timetable with
restaurants opening for lunch from noon to around 3
p.m., and dinner doesn't begin until 7 p.m. Since the
Italians usually don't eat until 9 p.m., it's advisable to
dine eat early to avoid the crowds and most likely
you'll also be dining with other tourists. (If you want
to eat with the locals, the later you eat, the better.)

Most of the restaurants located on the main
squares may offer great views but the better and less
expensive eateries are usually located on small streets
away from the bustling crowds. For the most part,
avoid restaurants that have waiters aggressively trying
to lure customers into their venue or passing out
flyers. The good restaurants don't need hawkers.

Once inside, don't expect the waitstaff to be as
friendly as waiters in America. Waiters are there to do
a job and will recite the specials, explain certain
dishes, and will even help you select a wine for your

meal. Italian menus are divided into courses. Italians often order one course at a time. They approach food in a much more relaxed and (some, including myself, would use the word "civilized") manner. They eat it and then order another course if they're still hungry. Don't look for a lot of those Italian dishes that you're use to seeing at your local Italian eatery at home because many are not authentic Italian so they won't be on any menu here in Rome. Personally, I always make a habit to asking for any specials if they are not offered because often they are some of the freshest and best dishes you can get. If there are specials, I always select one over anything on the menu. Always.

Getting the bill and tipping. Italians take their time eating and dining is never rushed. You may have to ask for the check as they consider it rude to drop down a check immediately after a meal is finished. Don't be surprised if it takes a good 15 minutes for the check to arrive after it has been requested. Note that in Rome, the waiters are paid a good wage and do not count on tips. Romans generally leave a euro per two people for a meal but many restaurants add a service charge so then you don't leave a tip. Tips should be left in cash because they don't offer an option to add a tip to a credit card charge.

Enjoy the sites of Rome, see the Coliseum, the Roman Forum, enjoy Sunday morning shopping at the Porta Portese flea market, toss a coin in the Trevi Fountain, and climb to the top of St. Peter's Basilica. Those things will all help work up an appetite but nothing gets your stomach churning more than the aromas in the air from the bakeries, the pizzerias, and the outdoor cafes. Eating authentic Italian cuisine is an experience and nothing like eating at your neighborhood Italian restaurant.

When in Rome, there are dishes that you can't leave without trying. Authentic Carbonara is the best and **Al Moro**, a restaurant located near the Trevi Fountain, is famous for its Carbonara. Italians rave about the deep fried crispy artichokes, so venture into the Jewish quarter and try this delicacy. The Italians are known for their pizza and they offer several varieties. Pizza Bianca, different than American pizza, is made with focaccia style pizza bread served in local bakeries. The Roman style thin crust pizza, not the pizza from Naples served mostly in the U.S., features a thin crust that's cooked crispy without the crust lip around the edges. While many American cities now feature gelato shops, they are nothing like authentic tartufo or gelato. Real Italian gelato is never fluffed up or disguised with artificial colors or chemicals. Tartufo, a popular dessert made famous by **Tre Scalini** in Piazza Navona, is a dessert made of one or two flavors with frozen fruit in the center and covered with a shell of chocolate.

It's true that Rome is overflowing with restaurants but like anywhere else in the world, many are overpriced, mediocre, and cater to unsuspecting tourists. Beware of the eateries that are filled with tourists only. Even in Rome you can order bad pizza and generic gelato.

Chapter 2

*The
A to Z Listings*

*Ridiculously Extravagant
Sensible Alternatives
Quality Bargain Spots*

ALFREDO ALLA SCROFA
Via della Scrofa 104A, Rome, +39 06 68806163
www.alfredoallascrofa.com
CUISINE: Italian/Mediterranean/Seafood
DRINKS: Full Bar
SERVING: Lunch & Dinner
PRICE RANGE: $$$
NEIGHBORHOOD: Centro Storico
This 1907 romantic eatery is known as the birthplace
of fettuccini Alfredo. Favorites: Fettuccine Alfredo
and Beef Carpaccio. Nice variety of wines.

ANTICO FORNO AI SERPENTI

Via dei Serpenti, 122-123, Rome, +39 06 4542 7920
www.anticofornoaiserpenti.it
CUISINE: Bakery
DRINKS: No Booze
SERVING: Breakfast & Lunch
PRICE RANGE: $$
NEIGHBORHOOD: Monti
With the atmosphere of a French bistro, this eatery offers baked goods and pizza. The treats include pies, cakes, panettone, puffs, and delicious espresso. If it's in season, get the pumpkin and gorgonzola panino. Popular among tourists, but not a tourist trap at all.

ARMANDO AL PANTHEON

Salita dè Crescenzi, 31, +39 06 6880 3034

www.armandoalpantheon.it

CUISINE: Roman

DRINKS: Full Bar

SERVING: Lunch, Dinner; closed Sun

PRICE RANGE: $$$

NEIGHBORHOOD: Centro Storico

This popular family run eatery offers a menu of classic and creative Roman cuisine. Some of the best traditional cooking you're going to find in Rome. Though it's right in what I would call "Tourist Trap Alley," don't let that fool you. Locals still come here in droves because the food's so good and they like the wood-paneled interior and wine list with fair prices. Vegetarian dishes are available. Menu favorites include Black rice with seafood, amatriciana, carbonara and Lasagna. Oh, let's not forget the *torta antic aroma*, a dish filled with fruit that's rather like strawberry shortcake, only better.

AROMA
PALAZZO MANFREDI HOTEL
Via Labicana, 125, Rome, +39 06 97615109
www.aromarestaurant.it
CUISINE: Modern Cuisine
DRINKS: Full Bar
SERVING: Lunch, Dinner
PRICE RANGE: $$$$
NEIGHBORHOOD: Esquilino
Located at Palazzo Manfredi Hotel, diners are treated to amazing views of Ancient Rome while enjoying the incredible cuisine of a 5-Diamond restaurant. Menu favorites include: Sea Bass and salmon duo with crispy king prawns and Chianina beef fillet in red wine. Impressive wine selection. An unforgettable dining experience.

AROMATICUS
Via Urbana, 134, 00184 Roma, +39 06 488 1355
www.aromaticus.it/
CUISINE: Juice Bar/Salads
DRINKS: Beer & Wine Only
SERVING: Lunch, Dinner; closed Mon
PRICE RANGE: $$$
NEIGHBORHOOD: Monti
This urban farming and aromatic herb shop sells
aromatic plants, edible flowers, sprouts, salts, exotic
peppers in the front of the house, while in the room at
the rear you'll find a little kitchen serving a menu of
salads, steak or fish tartare and Carpaccio. Select
wine selection.

BAFFETTO
Via del Governo Vecchio, 114, 00186 Roma, Italy
+39 06 686 1617
www.pizzeriabaffetto.it
CUISINE: Pizza

DRINKS: Beer & Wine Only
SERVING: Lunch Wed, Sat & Sun, Dinner nightly, closed Tuesday
PRICE RANGE: $$
NEIGHBORHOOD: Centro Storico
This little pizzeria features Roman-style, thin & crispy pizzas. Favorites include: Pizza marguerite and Pizza Baffetta. No Reservations. No cash.

BAR DEL FICO
Piazza del Fico 26, Rome, +39 06 68891373
www.bardelfico.com/en/
CUISINE: Café/Italian
DRINKS: Full Bar

SERVING: Breakfast, Lunch, & Dinner
PRICE RANGE: $$
NEIGHBORHOOD: Centro Storico/Parione
This funky eatery is one of Rome's hottest
restaurants. The place has a charming bar area and is
a popular late-night hangout. Affordable charcuterie
platters, smart cocktails. Reservations recommended.

C'È PASTA... E PASTA

Via Ettore Rolli, 29, +39 06 5832 0125
http://cepastaepasta.it
CUISINE: Bakery / Italian
DRINKS: No Booze
SERVING: Breakfast, Lunch & Dinner
PRICE RANGE: $
NEIGHBORHOOD: Trastevere
Nothing fancy about this cozy eatery serving
authentic Roman / Jewish Kosher cuisine. You can

translate the name of this place as "There's pasta… and pasta." Specialties: Lasagna & Ravioli and Sea Bass Carpaccio. Menu changes daily. There are certain dishes here that are popular among the Roman Jewish crowd—items like fried artichokes, battered fried cod, anchovy & frisee casserole. But I like them too. Fresh pasta shop where you can buy pasta to cook at home. Outdoor seating.

CACIO E PEPE

Via Giuseppe Avezzana 11, Rome, +39 06 3217268
www.trattoriacacioepepeprati.com
CUISINE: Italian
DRINKS: Beer & Wine Only
SERVING: Lunch & Dinner; Lunch only on Saturdays; closed Sundays
PRICE RANGE: $$
NEIGHBORHOOD: Prati
Intimate rustic (OK, it's definitely down market and kind of beat-up, but I love it) trattoria serving classic Italian fare. They have a handwritten menu, but opt for the signature dish that gives this place its name— *cacio e pepe* (basically, just cheese & black pepper, but unlike you've ever had it before unless you've been here). Other favorites: Bruchetta with ricotta cheese and Eggplant lasagna. Street dining on the heated sidewalk terrace for the ultimate Rome experience.

CAFÉ DONEY

Via Vittorio Veneto 125, Rome, +39 06 47082783
www.restaurantdoney.com
CUISINE: Italian

DRINKS: Beer & Wine Only
SERVING: Breakfast, Lunch & Dinner
PRICE RANGE: $$$
NEIGHBORHOOD: Termini
Casual but luxurious eatery offering creative menu of
Italian fare. Favorites: Roasted loin of rabbit and
Pasta with squid and cherry tomatoes. Nice wine
selection.

CASINE VALADIER

Piazza Bucarest, Rome, +39 06 6992 2090
www.casinavaladier.com
CUISINE: Italian
DRINKS: Full Bar
SERVING: Lunch & Dinner; closed Mon
PRICE RANGE: $$$$
Upscale Italian eatery featuring breathtaking views of
Rome from the terrace. Some have argued that this is
the best view in Rome, and I am not one to argue. It's
in a majestic villa next to the Borghese Gardens. The
view extends from the capacious balcony as well as
the ground-floor terrace from where you can get
spectacular views. Try to come here on a Sunday
where the brunch is long, leisurely and relaxing. (Plan
on two hours.) Though it's not always on the menu,
the chef's special dish (a fillet of beef with foie gras)
can always be ordered. Great desserts and wine
selection.

CESARE AL CASALETTO

Via del Casaletto, 45, +39 06 536015
http://www.trattoriadacesare.it
CUISINE: Italian / Pizza / Seafood
DRINKS: Full Bar
SERVING: Lunch & Dinner; Closed Wed
PRICE RANGE: $$
NEIGHBORHOOD: Gianicolense
Popular Italian eatery in a friendly elegant room
offering a menu of pastas, meats, and fish. Favorites:
Lamb Cacciatore and Eggplant meatballs, but they
have a suckling lamb that's very delicious, and so is
the delectable pasta alla gricia (cured pork jowl over a
pasta like rigatoni). Local wines from Italy, France
and Slovenia that are surprisingly cheap.
Reservations recommended.

CHECCHINO DAL 1887

Via di Monte Testaccio 30, Rome, +39 06 5743816
www.checchino-dal-1887.com
CUISINE: Roman
DRINKS: Beer & Wine Only
SERVING: Dinner; closed Mondays
PRICE RANGE: $$$
NEIGHBORHOOD: Ostiense, Testaccio
Beautiful refined eatery offering an upscale dining
experience. The friend who brought me here wanted
me to try the tripe with a soupy tomato mix, but I
draw the line at tripe. Can't stand the stuff. However,
I fell in love with the Bruschetta with pecorino &
sage and Oxtail. Impressive wine selection (quite a
few local wines, also) and rich desserts. Try the
Panna cotta – a cream custard with berry sauce.

COROMANDEL

Via di Monte Giordano 60, Rome, +39 06 68802461
www.coromandel.it

CUISINE: Brasseries
DRINKS: Full Bar
SERVING: Breakfast, Lunch, & Dinner; closed Mon
PRICE RANGE: $$$
NEIGHBORHOOD: Centro Storico
This cute little restaurant (with pale pink walls) offers a lovely décor and delicious food. This is one of the best spots for breakfast in the area. Nice selection of pizzas and you can order by the slice. The dinner menu is prix fixe, with excellent seasonal dishes like red snapper. The atmosphere is very relaxed, you can even read a book here without a complaint from the staff.

CRISTALLI DI ZUCCHERO

Via di Val Tellina 114, Rome, +39 06 58230323
https://www.ristorantevelavevodetto.it/prenota-quiriti-online.html
WEBSITE DOWN AT PRESSTIME
CUISINE: Bakery
DRINKS: Full Bar
SERVING: Breakfast/Brunch
PRICE RANGE: $$
NEIGHBORHOOD: Portuense
If you're in search of delicious sweets then you've found the place. The offerings include a variety of macaroons, cakes, cannolis, and a menu of tasty appetizers.

DA CESARE

Via del Casaletto 45, Rome, +39 06 536015
www.trattoriadacesare.it/?lang=en
CUISINE: Roman
DRINKS: Beer & Wine Only
SERVING: Lunch & Dinner; closed Wednesdays
PRICE RANGE: $$$
NEIGHBORHOOD: Portuense
Small neighborhood restaurant perched high upon a
hill, where people come for the food, definitely not
the décor. While the restaurant itself isn't much to
look at (and who cares anyway, right?), the views you
get up here are worth the trip. Favorites: Pasta alla
Gricia (best pasta in the world) and Eggplant
Croquettes (a great starter, like nothing you've ever
had before). I never leave without sampling their
superior fritto misto. Reservations recommended.

DA ENZO AL 29

Via dei Vascellari 29, Rome, +39 06 5812260
www.daenzoal29.com
CUISINE: Roman

DRINKS: Beer & Wine Only
SERVING: Lunch & Dinner; closed Sundays
PRICE RANGE: $$
NEIGHBORHOOD: Trastevere
A simple small eatery serving Roman classics.
Outdoor seating offers the best café experience
watching the crowds while dining. Favorites:
Fettucine with mussels and clams and Coda alla
vaccinara (Oxtail). Always a wait, but worth it.

DAL BOLOGNESE
Piazza del Popolo 1, Rome, +39 06 3222799
www.dalbolognese.it
CUISINE: Pizza, Mediterranean
DRINKS: Beer & Wine Only
SERVING: Lunch & Dinner; closed Mondays
PRICE RANGE: $$$$
NEIGHBORHOOD: Flaminio
Elegant restaurant serving high-end, expensive Italian
cuisine. Go upstairs to the smoking room where you
can also get a drink before dinner. Favorites:
Tagliatelle alla Bolognese and the Milanese (served
with pure mashed potatoes). Try their Tiramisu – a
different version that most serve. Nice wine selection.

DITIRANBO
Piazza della Cancelleria, 74-75, Rome, +39 06 687
1626
www.ristoranteditirambo.it
CUISINE: Italian
DRINKS: Beer & Wine Only
SERVING: Breakfast, Lunch, & Dinner
PRICE RANGE: $$$

NEIGHBORHOOD: Centro Storico
This small trattoria just a bit north of the Campo de'
Fiori offers a menu of seasonal and creative Roman
classics in a charming atmosphere with wood-beamed
ceilings. Here you'll find great antipasti and
unexpected treats like Gorgonzola-pear soufflé.
(Large vegetarian selection.) Menu favorites include:
Roast Lamb and Suckling pig. Impressive wine list of
over 500 labels.

EATALY
Piazzale XII Ottobre 1492, Rome, +39 06 90279201
www.roma.eataly.it
CUISINE: Italian
DRINKS: Full Bar
SERVING: Lunch, Dinner
PRICE RANGE: $$$
NEIGHBORHOOD: Ostiense
If you've been to their location in NYC, you know
what to expect...a food shrine to Italian cuisine. Here

you'll find pasta, wines, cheese, prosciutto, pesce, coffee, espresso, gelato, and more. Eat here or shop to take home. There are 4 or 5 aisles of just dried pasta. This location includes 23 restaurants, bakeries, a gelateria and a rosticceria.

ENOTECA FERRARA

Piazza Trilussa, 41, Rome, +39 06 5833 3920
www.enotecaferrara.it
CUISINE: Italian
DRINKS: Full Bar
SERVING: Lunch, Dinner
PRICE RANGE: $$$$
NEIGHBORHOOD: Trastevere

This upscale eatery offers an impressive menu of Italian fare, pretty rare in this neighborhood these days. Menu favorites include: Grilled Lamb chops and Homemade large chestnut fettuccine. This wine bar, restaurant and gastronomic boutique impress customers with its award-winning wine list.

ENOTECA L'ANTIDOTO
Vicolo del Bologna, 19, + 342 300 6808
https://www.facebook.com/enotecalantidoto/
CUISINE: Italian / Wine Bar
DRINKS: Wine
SERVING: Lunch & Dinner
PRICE RANGE: $

NEIGHBORHOOD: Centro / Trastevere
Small kitchen offering a simple menu of local favorites served at a counter & only a handful of high-top tables. You have to open wine yourself and pick up your menu selections from the kitchen counter window. Nice selection of wines. Wine shop. Don't let this form of serving put you off. It's something to do withb the restaurant licensing in rome. The staff are great, helping and fun. My Favoriutes: Figs & burrata; Porcini Mushroom Salad;

FELICE
Via Mastro Giorgio, 29, Rome, +39 06 574 6800
www.feliceatestaccio.it
CUISINE: Roman
DRINKS: Beer & Wine Only
SERVING: Lunch, Dinner

PRICE RANGE: $$$
NEIGHBORHOOD: Testaccio, Ostiense
Open since 1936, this celebrated trattoria features a
menu of authentic Roman pasta dishes and other
favorites. The food doesn't get more "traditional"
than it is here. Celebs like Roberto Benigni are
regulars, so they've been doing something right all
these years. The tables are packed tightly together, so
if you're claustrophobic, be warned! Menu highlights
include: Cacio e pepe and Amatriciana pasta. Get a
twist on the usual Carbonara by ordering the spaghetti
with cheese and pepper – they toss it right at your
table. The roasted lamb is superior. Reservations are a
must in this always-crowded place.

FIASCHETTERIA BELTRAMME
39 Via della Croce, Rome, +39 06 6979 7200
www.fiaschetteriabeltramme.info **WEBSITE
DOWN**
CUISINE: Italian
DRINKS: Full Bar
SERVING: Lunch & Dinner
PRICE RANGE: $$
Family restaurant featuring Italian classics, including
delicious homemade pastas, served in a very laid-
back homey atmosphere. I like the tonnarelli
especially. What sets this place apart is the great art
that hangs on the walls. It's a special dining
experience.

FLAVIO AI VELAVEVEDOTTO
Via di Monte Testaccio, 97, Rome, +39 06 574 4194
www.flavioalvelavevodetto.it
WEBSITE DOWN AT PRESS TIME
CUISINE: Roman
DRINKS: Beer & Wine Only
SERVING: Lunch, Dinner
PRICE RANGE: $$$
NEIGHBORHOOD: Testaccio, Ostiense
This unusual eatery is actually located in a centuries-old warehouse built into the "mountain of discarded clay pots," the city's most historic landfill. Menu highlights include: Cacio e Pepe, the Amatriciana, and the Carbonara, suckling pig, oxtail. Note: Menu is completely in Italian but the waitresses will make suggestions. Reservations recommended.

GINA
Via di San Sebastianello, 7A, Rome, +39 33 530 4277
https://ristoexpert.com/migliori-ristoranti/roma/gina

CUISINE: Italian
DRINKS: Full Bar
SERVING: Lunch, Dinner; closed
PRICE RANGE: $$$$
NEIGHBORHOOD: Parioli

GINA, a combination of the owner's names, offers a unique Italian eatery that promotes their passion for food. The menu features bruschetta, salads, sandwiches, pastries, gelato, and yogurt. In winter the restaurant offers fully stocked gourmet picnic baskets prepared for those headed to Villa Borghese Park.

GINGER

Via Borgognona, 43-44, Rome, +39 06 6994 0836
www.ginger.roma.it
CUISINE: Breakfast
DRINKS: Full Bar
SERVING: Breakfast & Lunch
PRICE RANGE: $$
NEIGHBORHOOD: Centro Storico

A nice alternative to the traditional trattoria, this Los Angeles-style eatery with its high-top marble tables and white tile décor offers a creative menu off baguette sandwiches, gnocchi, tortellini, smoothies, and homemade desserts. Here you'll also find an impressive variety of fresh fruit and vegetable juices. Menu available in English or Italian.

GLASS HOSTARIA

Vicolo Dè Cinque, Rome, +39 06 5833 5903
https://glasshostaria.it
CUISINE: Italian
DRINKS: Full Bar
SERVING: Dinner; closed Sun & Mon
PRICE RANGE: $$$$
NEIGHBORHOOD: Trastevere

Though it's in a Medieval building, the design of this slick and chic eatery is ultra-modern, and it offers an impressive upscale dining destination. A very with-it kind of crowd. Experimental items are featured, like risotto with saffron, wild fennel, anise and goat cheese; scallops with koji; rack of lamb with burnt onions and cherries. The tiramisu comes with chocolate crumble—like you've never had before.

GREEN T

Via del Piè di Marmo, 28, Rome, +39 06 679 8628
www.green-tea.it
CUISINE: Chinese
DRINKS: Beer & Wine Only
SERVING: Lunch, Dinner; closed Sun
PRICE RANGE: $$$
NEIGHBORHOOD: Centro Storico

This upscale Chinese restaurant offers and beautiful décor and great food. Menu favorites include: Sweet & Sour Pork and Peking Duck.

HIMALAYA PALACE
Circonvallazione Gianicolense, 277, + 06 582 6001
https://www.himalayapalace.com
CUISINE: Indian
DRINKS: Beer & Wine
SERVING: Lunch & Dinner; Dinner only on Mon, Lunch only on Sun
PRICE RANGE: $$
NEIGHBORHOOD: Portuense
Spacious eatery offering authentic Indian cuisine. Favorites: Fine Butter Chicken and Tandoori Prawns. Vegetarian and Gluten-Free options. Indoor/Outdoor seating.

IL CONVIVIO TROIANI

Vicolo dei Soldati, 31, +39 06 686 9432
http://www.ilconviviotroiani.it/
CUISINE: Italian
DRINKS: Beer & Wine Only
SERVING: Dinner; closed Sunday
PRICE RANGE: $$
NEIGHBORHOOD: Centro Storico
Beautiful eatery with a semi-private entrance (ring the doorbell) and you're welcomed into a lovely room filled with art and frescoes. Imaginative tasting menus. If you order a la carte, get the spaghetti with garlic and olive oil, spiced with chile, lemon, mint, almonds and pecorino. Unlike any spaghetti dish you've ever had, I promise.
Other menu picks: Squab liver in a cherry and Squab consommé. Nice wine pairings.

IL MARGUTTA

Via Margutta, 118, Rome, +39 06 3265 0577
www.ilmargutta.bio
CUISINE: Vegetarian
DRINKS: Beer & Wine Only
SERVING: Lunch, Dinner; open daily
PRICE RANGE: $$$
NEIGHBORHOOD: Flaminio
This unique eatery features a café and bar with a
buffet area located between the two. Food varies from
Greek, Indian and Italian. Nice vegetarian options.
Great spot for brunch or lunch. This place is also an
art gallery.

IL PAGLIACCIO

Via dei Banchi Vecchi 129A, Rome, +39 06
68809595
www.ristoranteilpagliaccio.com

CUISINE: Italian
DRINKS: Full Bar
SERVING: Lunch, Dinner
PRICE RANGE: $$$$
NEIGHBORHOOD: Centro Storico
Chef/owner Anthony Genovese offers a menu of true
Roman cuisine served in an attractive intimate space.
Menu favorites include great pastas and fish dishes.
The desserts are quite creative like the brown bread
ice cream and caramel chocolate truffle. Impressive
wine menu offers more that 500 labels. Advance book
of a month prior required.

IL SORPASSO
31 Via Properzia, Rome, +39 06 8902 4554
www.sorpasso.info
CUISINE: Italian
DRINKS: Full Bar
SERVING: Breakfast & Lunch; closed Sundays
PRICE RANGE: $
NEIGHBORHOOD: Prati
A short walk from the Vatican is this favorite where
locals hang out after work. Filled with neighborhood
regulars who come for the cheap wine and cheap
Italian favorites. Go by for lunch and get a charcuterie
board featuring some of the in-house cured meats and
wide selection of cheeses.

IL TEMPIO DI ISIDE

11 Via Pietro Verri, Rome, +39 06 700 4741
www.isideristorante.it
CUISINE: Mediterranean
DRINKS: Full Bar
SERVING: Lunch & Dinner
PRICE RANGE: $$$$
Only a few minutes' walk from the Colosseum. It
may be listed in some publications as a tourist spot,
this is also a locals' favorite. The owners go every
morning to the local "fish auction" to get the freshest
catch. Menu picks include: Fried baby octopus'
tentacles and Langoustine and Prawn. Nice selection
of wine. Reservations recommended.

IL VERO ALFREDO

Piazza Augusto Imperatore 30, Rome, +39 06
6878734
www.ilveroalfredo.it
CUISINE: Italian
DRINKS: Full Bar
SERVING: Lunch & Dinner, Dinner only on
Mondays
PRICE RANGE: $$$
NEIGHBORHOOD: Centro Storico

Known as the birthplace of Fettuccine Alfredo
(though there are other places that claim credit), their
version is made with housemade pasta and is creamy
and well flavored. People travel the world to sample
the Fettuccine Alfredo here. Also impressive is the
famous "gold cutlery" donated in 1927 by actors
Mary Pickford and Douglas Fairbanks. I send people
here to get the experience, but I don't go here myself
anymore. Very expensive.

IVO
Via di San Francesco a Ripa 158, Rome, +39 06
5817082
https://ivoatrastevere.it
CUISINE: Italian/Pizza
DRINKS: Full Bar
SERVING: Dinner, Lunch also on Saturday closed
Tuesdays
PRICE RANGE: $$
NEIGHBORHOOD: Trastevere

Simple pizzeria serving Roman-style pizzas. Very unassuming but you're here for the pizzas. Nice pasta dishes as well, but skip them for the pizza. Fair to good wine selection.

L'ARCANGELO
Via Giuseppe Gioachino Belli, +39 06 3210992
www.larcangelo.com/
CUISINE: Italian
DRINKS: Full bar
SERVING: Lunch/Dinner/Late Night; closed Sunday
PRICE RANGE: $$$
NEIGHBORHOOD: Prati
Nice upscale eatery with a menu that includes English translations of each dish. Great Italian fare and they are known for serving the best Gnocchi (with Amatriciana sauce) in Rome. (Well, one of the top 10, anyway.) There's also this very flavorful salad: Viaggio a Rocca Priora, which refers to a trip to the chef's hometown—it's got mixed greens wth poached egg spiced with fennel, cumin, licorice. For dessert, I heartily recommend the Beignets Stuffed with Citrus Custard and Caramel. Reservations recommended.

LA BUVETTE

44 Via Vittoria, Rome, +39 06 679 0383
https://dbs-restaurants.com/
CUISINE: Italian/Breakfast
DRINKS: No Booze
SERVING: Breakfast, Lunch & Dinner
PRICE RANGE: $$$

On a quiet side street is this endearing café, a traditional old world eatery featuring classic local Italian dishes with sidewalk seating you'll want to take advantage of in good weather. Nice wine pairings.

LA CAMPANA

Vicolo della Campana 18, Rome, +39 06 6875273
www.ristorantelacampana.com
CUISINE: Roman
DRINKS: Full Bar

SERVING: Dinner; closed Mondays
PRICE RANGE: $$
NEIGHBORHOOD: Centro Storico
Known as the oldest restaurant in Rome (dating to
1518), so dining here is definitely an experience not
to be rushed. Family-friendly food (and prices).
Favorites: Roasted chicken and Pasta ai carciofi
(pasta with artichokes).

LA MONTECARLO

Vicolo Savelli, 13, Rome, +39 06 686 1877
www.lamontecarlo.it
CUISINE: Pizza
DRINKS: Full Bar
SERVING: Lunch, Dinner; closed Sun
PRICE RANGE: $$
NEIGHBORHOOD: Trastevere
Popular with locals, this pizzeria offers an impressive
variety of thin-crust pizza, pastas, bruschetta, and
canapés. Favorites include the Parma Prosciutto Pizza
and Wild Mushroom Fettuccini. Desserts are
homemade.

LA PERGOLA
Via Alberto Cadlolo, 101, Rome, +39 06 3509 2152
www.romecavalieri.it
CUISINE: Italian
DRINKS: Full Bar
SERVING: Lunch, Dinner; closed Mon
PRICE RANGE: $$$$
NEIGHBORHOOD: Balduina/Montemario
Known as one of the best restaurants in Rome boasting a three-Michelin star rating, this popular eatery also features a wine cellar with over 60,000 bottles. Menu favorites include: Ravioli stuffed with carbonara sauce and Cod with broccoli and salt cod snow. The stunning view alone is worth the visit.

LA FOCACCIA
Via della Pace, 11, Rome, +39 06 9761 7557
www.1stmuse.com/focaccia

CUISINE: Italian/Pizza
DRINKS: Full Bar
SERVING: Lunch, Dinner
PRICE RANGE: $$
NEIGHBORHOOD: Centro Storico
Decorated with exposed brickwork and beamed ceilings, this casual eatery offers more than the great wood-fired pizzas. Here you'll also find delicious pasta and roasted meat dishes, all under the looming edifice of Bramante's gorgeous Santa Maria della Pace church. Whenever visitors drag me into the church so they can have a well-deserved look, I bring them here afterwards. They all love it.

LA TAVERNE DEI FORI IMPERIALI
Via della Madonna dei Monti, 9, Rome, +39 06 679 8643
www.latavernadeiforiimperiali.com
CUISINE: Italian
DRINKS: Beer & Wine Only
SERVING: Lunch, Dinner
PRICE RANGE: $$
NEIGHBORHOOD: Monti, Centro Storico
Located in the center of Rome, this traditional eatery is known for its menu of classic and creative home-cooked pastas and grilled dishes. It's the kind of locals' place where you trust them so much you always order the daily special. Ask them what they recommend, and then take it. Favorites include: Carbonara, Scaloppini with ham and sage, and Noodles with bacon, zucchini and cheese (to die for). Impressive list of Italian wines.

LA TERRAZZA

Via Ludovisi, 49, Rome, +39 06 4781 2752
www.dorchestercollection.com/en/rome/hotel-eden/restaurants-bars/la-terrazza/
CUISINE: Italian
DRINKS: Full Bar
SERVING: Lunch, Dinner; open daily
PRICE RANGE: $$$$
NEIGHBORHOOD: Centro Storico
This eatery, a tourist favorite, offers a beautiful
panoramic view of Rome. Menu includes lobster,
lamb, steak, and antipasto. Great wine selection.
Jackets required.

LA TRADIZIONE

Via Cipro, 8 E, + 06 3972 0349
https://latradizione.it/index.html
CUISINE: Cheese Shop
DRINKS: Beer & Wine
SERVING: Lunch & Dinner; Closed Sun
PRICE RANGE: $$$
NEIGHBORHOOD: Prati, Balduina/Montemario
Cheese shop selling more than 400 cheeses, but a whole lot more, with a nice selection of cured meats, prepared foods, and other gourmet products. Though this is considered one of the top 3 or 4 high quality suppliers in all of Rome, the prices are more than reasonable for what you're getting, trust me. I once stayed in an AirBnB for 4 days nearby, and came here every day for food. I think one reason for the low prices is its location in a working-class district. Quiet place for an expresso or café au latte with a pastry.

LE MANI IN PASTA
Via dei Genovesi 37, Rome, +39 06 5816017
www.ristorantedipescetrastevere.roma.it
CUISINE: Italian
DRINKS: Beer & Wine Only
SERVING: Lunch, Dinner; closed Mon
PRICE RANGE: $$$$
NEIGHBORHOOD: Trastevere
This popular rustic eatery offers a menu of classic
Italian fare including fresh pastas. Menu favorites
include: Tuna tartare, Brasaole with buffalo
mozzarella and small gnocchi with clams. Delicious
selection of desserts. Reservations recommended
because the place is so small. Getting turned away
twice because I decided to stop by at the last minute
cured me. Now I always book a table. Oh, and ask for
a table upstairs or you'll be sent to the basement
people can smoke.

LITRO
Via Fratelli Bonnet, 5, +39 06 4544 7639
CUISINE: Italian
DRINKS: Full bar
SERVING: Dinner; Closed Sunday
PRICE RANGE: $$
NEIGHBORHOOD: Monteverde Vecchio
Nice laid back wine bar offering amazing food and
wine. It's a small place with only about 20 seats
inside, but there's outdoor seating as well. Some
people come just for their "natural" wine, but I'm not
one of them. It's the food here that stands out. The
artichokes are splendid. Usually, in most Roman
restaurants, they're either deep-fried or cooked with

olive oil. Here, though, the chef serves them the way they do in villages around Italy: thinly sliced raw and sprinkled simply with olive oil & lemon. Nothing beats it. I had 2 orders of this last time I visited.

MA CHE SIETE VENUTI A FÀ
Via Benedetta, 25, +39 06 6456 2046
https://www.football-pub.com
CUISINE: Pub
DRINKS: Full Bar
SERVING: Lunch & Dinner
PRICE RANGE: $$
NEIGHBORHOOD: Centro
Popular watering hole known for its selection of Italian artisan ales and beers on tap (and a

discriminating selection in the bottle). It's been here quite a while, and has a loyal following. The 10 to 15 beers on tap rotate constantly, and come from the US, the UK, Germany, Belgium, Italy of course (which has lots of excellent brews). Hold out for a table outside on the street so you can enjoy the bustling nightlife crowds surging to and fro in Trastevere. Simple menu of pub grub.

MACCHERCONI

Piazza delle Coppelle, 44, Rome, +39 06 6830 7895
www.ristorantemaccheroni.com
CUISINE: Roman
DRINKS: Full Bar
SERVING: Lunch, Dinner; open daily
PRICE RANGE: $$
NEIGHBORHOOD: Centro Storico

Not far from the Pantheon you'll find this relaxed eatery offering a menu of homemade Roman cuisine. The place is decorated like an old Roman apartment, with nothing really matching. You'll feel like you're in someone's home. Menu highlights include: Steak, Tripa (a classic Roman dish), and Gnocchi with gorgonzola and pear. Try the tonnarelli, a large type of spaghetti.

MARZAPANE

Via Velletri, 39, +39 06 6478 1692
www.marzapaneroma.com/
CUISINE: Italian
DRINKS: Full bar
SERVING: Lunch/Dinner; Closed Wednesday
PRICE RANGE: $$$$
NEIGHBORHOOD: Pinciano

Chef Alba Ruiz offers customers three different menus (6, 8 and 9 courses). Excellent food with a long list of glowing reviews to prove it. Do try the Spanish-born chef's risotto—it's very different from what you get elsewhere. While most cooks use olive oil for everything, here they use butter, French butter, and the Cantabrian anchovies in the risotto are beyond flavorful.

MOSTÒ

Viale Pinturicchio, 32, + 392 257 9616
https://m.facebook.com/enotecamosto/
CUISINE: Wine Bar / Italian
DRINKS: Full Bar
SERVING: Dinner; Closed on Mon
PRICE RANGE: $$

NEIGHBORHOOD: Flaminio
Intimate wine bar on a very quiet street off the beaten path serving a small assortment of simple dishes. The wine is the star here, with an emphasis on "natural wine." Popular dish: Buffalo Mozzarella which the owner gets fresh from Campania. It's near the MAXXI Museum for Contemporary Art.

MUSEO-ATELIER CANOVA TADOLINI

150A-B Via del Babuino, Rome, +39 06 3211 0702
www.canovatadolini.com
CUISINE: Italian
DRINKS: Full Bar
SERVING: Lunch, Late Night, Dinner, Breakfast, Reservations
PRICE RANGE: $$$$
Elegant museum café with a menu of pizzas, finger foods, and pastas. Menu picks include: Tuna steak and Chicken with pistachio. Great place for cocktails before or after a museum visit.

NO.AU

Piazza di Montevecchio, 17, Rome, +39 06 4565 2770
www.noauroma.wordpress.com
CUISINE: Italian
DRINKS: Full Bar
SERVING: Dinner, Late night
PRICE RANGE: $$$
NEIGHBORHOOD:
This tiny bistro serves over 100 varieties of beer. The small menu features bar snacks, steak tartare, and cheese plates. Reservations recommended.

NONNA BETTA

Via del Portico d'Ottavia 16, Rome, +39 06 68806263
www.nonnabetta.it
CUISINE: Jewish, Roman, Middle Eastern
DRINKS: Full Bar
SERVING: Lunch & Dinner; closed Tuesday
PRICE RANGE: $$
NEIGHBORHOOD: Centro Storico
Elegant Italian/Kosher restaurant decorated "old world-style". Favorites: Lasagna with artichokes and Carbonara alla giudia (carbonara Jewish style). Great selection of authentic Jewish cuisine. Don't leave without trying the Jewish style fried artichoke, with its crispy petals and soft pulpy meat.

OPEN BALADIN

Via degli Specchi 6, +39 06 6838989
www.openbaladinroma.it

CUISINE: Burgers
DRINKS: Beer & Wine Only
SERVING: Lunch, Dinner
PRICE RANGE: $$
NEIGHBORHOOD: Centro Storico
This place is actually a pub serving over 100 bottled beers and 40 draught Italian beers. The ever-changing menu includes a wide variety of treats including made-to-order potato chips. The bar grub served here has an American slant: buffalo style chicken wings.

OSTERIA LA GENSOLE
Piazza della Gensola, 15, +39 06 581 6312
www.osterialagensola.it
CUISINE: Roman/Seafood
DRINKS: Beer & Wine Only
SERVING: Lunch, Dinner
PRICE RANGE: $$$
NEIGHBORHOOD: Trastevere
This popular (and still family-run) eatery offers Sicilian fare that makes dining an adventure. The seafood themed menu offers a wide variety of items like the sea bass "ceviche," Carbonara, and fresh tuna "meatballs." Also popular is the spaghetti with sea urchin. Try the tasting menu for a treat.

OTALEG

Via di S. Cosimato, 14a, + 338 651 5450
https://www.otaleg.com
CUISINE: Ice Cream / Gelato
DRINKS: No Booze
SERVING: 12 – 9 p.m., noon to midnight on Fri &
Sat
PRICE RANGE: $$
NEIGHBORHOOD: Trastevere
Small gelato/ice cream shop offering a selection of
flavors from vanilla to the exotic. It also happens to
be some of the best rich and creamy gelati you can
get in Italy. This is owing to their use of only the
finest ingredients, such as Valrhona and Amedici
chocolates and Romana hazelnuts. While the fruit,
chocolate and nut sorbets ought to be tried, Pistachio
gelato is still my personal favorite. Vegan options.

PASTICCERIA BOCCIONE

Via del Portico D'Ottavia, +39 06 687 8637
No Website
CUISINE: Kosher Bakery/Desserts
DRINKS: No Booze
SERVING: Breakfast & Lunch; closed Sat & Sun
PRICE RANGE: $$
NEIGHBORHOOD: Centro Storico
This Kosher bakery offers an impressive selection
desserts including Ricotta cake, plum marmalade and
almond crème cake, and dried-fruit cake. You'll also
find an assortment of cookies, macaroons, biscotti,

pies, and sweet pizza. Note: most of the fresh pastries
sell out by late morning.

PASTIFICIO SAN LORENZO

Via Tiburtina 196, 00199 Rome, +39 06 504 2669
www.pastificiosanlorenzo.com/
CUISINE: Italian
DRINKS: Beer & Wine Only
SERVING: Lunch & Dinner, Dinner only on
Saturdays: closed Sundays

PRICE RANGE: $$$
NEIGHBORHOOD: San Lorenzo
Located in a former pasta factory close to the main
train station is this upscale dining with an open
kitchen. It is part of the Fondazione Cerere, which
gives working space to artists—this restaurant and bar
is part of their headquarters. Impressive selection of
wines – mostly from local wineries. Atmosphere is
very nice and there's a hipness to the feel in this
place.

PERILLI
Via Marmorata, 39, Rome, +39 06 575 5100
www.perilliatestaccio.com/
CUISINE: Roman/Italian
DRINKS: Full Bar
SERVING: Lunch, Dinner; closed Wed
PRICE RANGE: $$$

NEIGHBORHOOD: Testaccio, Ostiense
Open since 1911, this old style Italian eatery offers special dishes like stewed Roman artichokes and Rigatoni Carbonara (the restaurant's most popular dish). This eatery serves delicious interpretations of classic Italian dishes. Nice wine selection. Bring somebody who speaks Italian or plan on pointing to something on the menu.

PESCHERIA OSTERIA SOR DUILIO

Via delle Cave di Pietralata 44, Rome, +39 06 41787439
www.pescheriasorduilio.com
CUISINE: Seafood
DRINKS: Beer & Wine Only
SERVING: Breakfast, Lunch, & Dinner; closed Mon, Thurs & Sat
PRICE RANGE: $$

NEIGHBORHOOD: Montesacro/Talenti
Not really a restaurant but a fish market that serves raw fish. There's a counter with fish to buy like raw oysters, sushi, and sashimi. Make a reservation if you want a table.

PIATTO ROMANO

Via Giovanni Battista Bodoni 62, Rome, +39 06 64014447
www.piattoromano.com
CUISINE: Roman
DRINKS: Beer & Wine Only
SERVING: Dinner
PRICE RANGE: $$$
NEIGHBORHOOD: Ostiense, Testaccio
Simply decorated eatery offering a limited menu of traditional Roman dishes. Menu picks: Polpette (small meatballs), Lamb sweetbreads, sweet & salty baked cod fish and delicious sautéed anchovies. All the pastas are top-notch. Delicious freshly baked focaccia bread. Not a tourist spot, but English is spoken here.

PIERLUIGI

Piazza de' Ricci 144, Rome, +39 06 6868717
www.pierluigi.it
CUISINE: Italian
DRINKS: Beer & Wine Only
SERVING: Lunch & Dinner, Lunch only on
Saturdays; closed Mondays
PRICE RANGE: $$$$
NEIGHBORHOOD: Centro Storico
Authentic Italian eatery offering traditional dishes
with an emphasis on seafood specialties prepared
perfectly. Favorites: Pasta Carbonara and Prawns
carpaccio. Great dining on the terrace overlooking the
piazza, where, thankfully, cars re not allowed.
Impressive 600 label wine cellar. Heavenly desserts.

PIPERNO

Via Monte de' Cenci 9. Rome, +39 06 68806629

www.ristorantepiperno.it
CUISINE: Roman/Kosher
DRINKS: Beer & Wine Only
SERVING: Lunch & Dinner, Lunch only on
Saturdays; closed Mondays
PRICE RANGE: $$$
NEIGHBORHOOD: Centro Storico
This places dates back to 1860, before Italy was even
a country, and is a high-end Jewish restaurant (but try
to sit outside because it's so nice) serving classic
dishes in an old-world setting. Favorites: Gnocchi alla
fontina and Bresaola Della Casa. Try the Jewish-style
artichoke – you won't be disappointed. Impressive
wine list.

PIZZERIA REMO

44 Piazza di Santa Maria Liberatrice, Rome, +39 06
5746270
No Website
CUISINE: Pizza
DRINKS: Beer & Wine Only
SERVING: Dinner, closed Sundays
PRICE RANGE: $$
Popular pizzeria that serves some of the best wood-
fired pizza in Rome. Great margarita pizza, eggplant
parmesan and fried arancini. Outdoor tables. Cash
only. Short wait. Very little English spoken here. but
it's always at the top of the "10 best" lists. You'll see
why.

PIZZARIUM

Via della Meloria 43, Rome, +39 06 39745416
www.bonci.it

CUISINE: Pizza
DRINKS: Beer & Wine Only
SERVING: Lunch, Dinner
PRICE RANGE: $$
NEIGHBORHOOD: Balduina/Montemario, Prati
This pizzeria offers a great variety (including pizza
with almonds and melon) and the pizza is sold per
pound. They use a 100-year-old sourdough starter.
Different flours are used as well, like kamut and
enkir. This is a take-out place so be prepared to stand
if you want to eat here.

QUINZI E GABRIELI
Via Delle Coppelle, Rome, +39 06 6879389
www.quinziegabrieli.it
CUISINE: Seafood
DRINKS: Full Bar

SERVING: Lunch, Dinner; closed Sun & Mon
PRICE RANGE: $$$$
NEIGHBORHOOD: Centro Storico
This elegant high-end eatery attracts power players
wearing suits because it's close to the parliament and
government buildings. The waiter begins pouring
champagne before you even sit at the table. It offers
an impressive and elaborate seafood-based menu.
There are three beautifully decorated rooms. Guests
can order a la carte or select from a prix fixe menu.
Try the cuttlefish with crunchy artichokes or one of
the many excellent lobster dishes available.

RISTORANTE NINO

11 Via Borgognona, Rome, +39 06 678 6752
www.ristorantenino.it
CUISINE: Italian/Tuscan
DRINKS: Full Bar
SERVING: Lunch & Dinner; closed Wednesdays
PRICE RANGE: $$$$
Upscale Italian eatery specializing in Tuscan dishes.
Try the ribollita (a belly-filling bread-and-vegetable
soup), the crostini with liver paté. Great classics like
Eggplant parmigiana and homemade ravioli. If you
want dessert, get the chestnut cake. Nice selection of
wines from the owner's estate.

RISTORANTE PIPERNO

Via Monte Dè Cenci, 9, Rome, +39 06 6880 6629
www.ristorantepiperno.it
CUISINE: Roman
DRINKS: Beer & Wine Only
SERVING: Lunch, Dinner

PRICE RANGE: $$$
NEIGHBORHOOD: Centro Storico
This high-end Jewish eatery offers a menu of classic
Roman dishes in an old world setting. Menu
highlights include: Jewish-style artichokes (an Italian
classic) and Spaghetti with clams. Popular choice for
Sunday lunch.

ROSCIOLI

Via dei Giubbonari, 21, +39 06 6875287
http://www.salumeriaroscioli.com/
CUISINE: Italian
DRINKS: Beer & Wine Only
SERVING: Dinner; closed Sunday
PRICE RANGE: $$
NEIGHBORHOOD: Centro Storico
Formerly a family grocer, now a multipurpose
gourmet bodega complete with a wine cellar offering
over 2,800 Italian and international wines. Menu

features classic Italian dishes with a twist like "brick dough dumplings" and Burrata with caviar. The delicious carbonara is considered by many people to be the best in Rome. Plan to reserve 4 weeks out.

ROSATI
Piazza del Popolo 4/5a, Rome, +39 06 322 5859
www.rosatibar.it
CUISINE: Italian
DRINKS: Full Bar
SERVING: Breakfast, Lunch & Dinner
PRICE RANGE: $$$
NEIGHBORHOOD: Flaminio
High-end art deco Italian restaurant & chocolatiers dating back to the 1920s. Definitely a dining experience as the waiters all wear white tuxedos with white gloves. Favorites: Spaghetti with clams and Tagliatelle with mushrooms. While the best seats are at the outdoor tables overlooking the square, you'll

find the Negronis cost 3 times as much in those seats as they do at the inside bar. Nice wine selection.

ROSTI AL PIGNETO

Via Bartolomeo d'Alviano, 65, Rome, +39 06 275 2608
www.rostialpigneto.it
CUISINE: Italian/Burgers
DRINKS: Full Bar
SERVING: Lunch weekends, Dinner nightly
PRICE RANGE: $$
NEIGHBORHOOD: Pigneto
This unique and hip "cooking lab" and Chef Marco Gallotta welcome trendy guests to taste the results of the agricultural research and kitchen. Menu includes veggies, ultra-thin-crust pizzas, 6 variations on the burger, pastas and delicious homemade desserts.

SAID

Via Tiburtina 135, Rome, 39 06 445 9204
www.said.it
CUISINE: Chocolatiers/Desserts
DRINKS: Full Bar
SERVING: Breakfast, Lunch, & Dinner
PRICE RANGE: $$
NEIGHBORHOOD: San Lorenzo
Located in an old chocolate factory, this unique restaurant offers a delicious chocolate-themed menu. Menu highlights include: Tartare with dark chocolate and Tonnarelli with shavings of truffle. Of course there's a large selection of chocolate desserts and sweets to select from.

SBANCO

Via Siria, 1, +39 06 789318
https://sbanco.eatbu.com
CUISINE: Pizza/Italian
DRINKS: Beer & Wine Only
SERVING: Dinner; Closed Monday
PRICE RANGE: $$
NEIGHBORHOOD: Appio San Giovanni

Popular eatery serving great pizzas and Italian fare.
I've never been as mad about pizzas (even very good
ones) as most Americans, but some friends *dragged*
me here, insisting
I had to taste the pizza. (It's rated as one of the top
pizza places in all of Rome.) The chef's secret is his
domed wood-burning Valoriana oven that keeps the
temperature hotter than other ovens. Before baking
the dough, he sprinkles little pieces of ice over it.
When the oven melts the ice, the surface of the pizza
is left wet and a little sticky. OK, it was good. But

personally, I like thin-crust pizza. Nice variety of
craft beers and local wines.

SETTEMBRINI CAFÉ
Via Luigi Settembrini, 27, Rome, +(39)3232617
www.viasettembrini.it
CUISINE: Italian

DRINKS: Full Bar
SERVING: Breakfast, Lunch, & Dinner
PRICE RANGE: $$$$
NEIGHBORHOOD: Prati
The chef's tasting course is a great choice in this upscale modern eatery (with oak plank floors and intimate tables) as it includes treats like raw sea bass with chopped fruit, a sea urchin gelato, rigatoni with anchovies, and seared duck with carrot puree. They offer a buffet lunch, afternoon tea, and full dinner service. Locals who know their wines come here because the extensive selections by the glass are excellent. Perfect place to sit outside in the summer.

SETTIMIO ALL'ARANCIO
Via dell'Arancio, 50, Rome, +39 06 687 6119
www.settimioallarancio.it
CUISINE: Italian
DRINKS: Full Bar
SERVING: Lunch, Dinner; closed Sun
PRICE RANGE: $$$
NEIGHBORHOOD: Centro Storico

This Italian eatery serves their meals family style. It draws people in the media as well as the art world. Italian eateries are not known for their steaks but this one serves delicious steaks like the T-Bone Steak Roman Style. If it's fish you want, get the moist whole fish baked in salt. Dessert selections include a tasty homemade tiramisu.

SETTIMIO AL PELLEGRINO
117 Via del Pellegrino, Rome, +39 06 68801978
www.settimioalpellegrinoroma.it
CUISINE: Italian
DRINKS: Beer & Wine Only
SERVING: Lunch & Dinner; closed Wednesdays
PRICE RANGE: $$
NEIGHBORHOOD: Centro Storico
Charming mom & pop eatery offering a limited menu of Italian classics in two small rooms – one looks into the kitchen. Pop runs the front. Mom runs the kitchen. When I say "limited menu," I mean it. You have to choose from whatever Mom wants to cook that day— usually, you'll get a choice of a couple of pastas and a meat dish and a fish selection. If they have it the day you visit, get the stracciatella (an egg soup that's really special). Favorites: Fettucine with meat sauce and Gnocchi with tomato sauce. Save room for their special dessert - a slice of super sweet Mont Blanc (chestnut and mascarpone meringue). Reservations recommended.

SFORNO

Via Statilio Ottato, 110-116, Rome, +39 06 7154
6118
www.sforno.it
CUISINE: Pizza
DRINKS: Beer & Wine Only
SERVING: Dinner, closed Sun
PRICE RANGE: $$
NEIGHBORHOOD: Tuscolano
This popular eatery offers a great selection of pizzas,
fried foods and desserts all homemade. Try the cacao
e pepe pizza that's topped with lots of black pepper
and a thick layer of pecorino cheese. Great assortment
of craft beers.

SUPPLIZIO

Via Dei Banchi Vecchi 143, +39 06 8987 1920
https://www.facebook.com/SupplizioRoma/
CUISINE: Italian / Tapas
DRINKS: Full Bar
SERVING: Lunch & Dinner; Closed Sun
PRICE RANGE: $$$
NEIGHBORHOOD: Centro Storico
Popular casual eatery by a famous chef serving
classic Roman street food like suppli (rice balls),
potato croquettes, anchovy meatballs, and the best,
crema fritta (pastry cream). Meat and vegetarian
options. Order at the counter, living room seating.
Daily specials.

TAVERNACCIA DA BRUNO

Via Giovanni da Castel Bolognese, 63, +39 06 581 2792

https://www.latavernacciaroma.com

CUISINE: Roman/Pizza

DRINKS: Beer & Wine

SERVING: Lunch & Dinner; Closed Wed

PRICE RANGE: $$

NEIGHBORHOOD: Trastevere

Cozy tavern offering homestyle dishes. Favorites: Roasted suckling pig cooked in the wood-fired oven; on Sunday they have Lasagna with homemade pasta (get there early because whatever they made for the day always sells out). Handwritten menus. Vegetarian options. Impressive wine selection.

TRAPIZZINO

Piazza Trilussa, 46, + 06 581 7312
https://www.trapizzino.it
CUISINE: Italian / Pizza
DRINKS: Beer & Wine
SERVING: Lunch & Dinner
PRICE RANGE: $
NEIGHBORHOOD: Trastevere
Part of a popular chain (they even have one in New York, or used to) serving street food. Classic street food pizza sold by the weight. "Trapizzino" combines the triangular tramezzino sandwich with pizza dough, almost like a pita pocket—filled with various choices like oxtail with tomato & celery; chicken cacciatore. Chesp, fast and filling. Other locations offer only counter service, but this one has table with full service. Great breakfast spot. Vegetarian options. Nice wine selection.

TRATTORIA AL MORO

Vicolo delle Bollette, 13, Rome, +39 06 678 3495
www.ristorantealmororoma.com
CUISINE: Italian
DRINKS: Full Bar
SERVING: Lunch, Dinner; closed Wed & Sun
PRICE RANGE: $$$

NEIGHBORHOOD: Centro Storico
Near the Pantheon and around the corner from the
Trevi Fountain is this high-end, wood-paneled
restaurant dating back to the late 1920s that has a
classic Roman menu with an impressive wine list that
attracts a Who's Who of VIPs in Rome. It's better to
come here with someone from Rome if you can
arrange that. The extensive menu is in Italian but the
waiter will assist. Here you'll find a great selection of
homemade pastas and sauces like the special Al Moro
pasta with spicy lamb. Look for anything made with
ovoli, a hard-to-find mushroom. It's delicious.

TRATTORIA DA LUCIA

Vicolo del Mattonato, 2, +39 06 580 3601
CUISINE: Roman
DRINKS: Beer & Wine Only
SERVING: Lunch, Dinner
PRICE RANGE: $$
NEIGHBORHOOD: Trastevere
This place is popular with both locals and tourists (the
food is so good the locals put up with the tourists.
You have to walk a bit to get here. This trattoria
offers up a menu of Roman specialties. My favorite is
the Omelet with Parmesan cheese—that's all there is
to it, but somehow it's miraculous. Other highlights
include Trippa all romana (Tripe with tomato sauce)
and Pollo con peperoni (chicken with peppers). , Save
room for dessert for they serve what is possibly
Rome's best tiramisu. **Cash only**.

TRATTORIA VECCHIA ROMA

Via Ferruccio 12B, Rome, +39 06 4467143

www.trattoriavecchiaroma.it
CUISINE: Italian
DRINKS: Beer & Wine Only
SERVING: Lunch, Dinner; closed Sun
PRICE RANGE: $$
NEIGHBORHOOD: Esquilino
This intimate trattoria offers a menu of classic Italian fare including a variety of bruschettas and pastas. Menu favorites include the tasty Spaghetti Parmigiana.

URBANA 47
Via Urbana, 47, Rome, +39 06 4788 4006
www.urbana47.it
CUISINE: Italian
DRINKS: Full Bar
SERVING: Lunch, Dinner
PRICE RANGE: $$$
NEIGHBORHOOD: Monti

This unique food project unites people in the name of food that celebrates the heritage of the Lazio region. A good way to try the food here is to check out the cocktail hour buffet. Menu includes tapas, pastas, salads, organic lamb, and vegetarian dishes, pumpkin ravioli, fresh pecorino. A favorite of foodies with its impressive ever-changing menu. (They even list the names of their suppliers on the menu.) It's definitely a culinary experience.

ZIA RESTAURANT
Via Goffredo Mameli, 45, + 06 2348 8093
https://ziarestaurant.com/en/
CUISINE: Italian
DRINKS: Full Bar
SERVING: Dinner, Lunch & Dinner Fri & Sat;
Closed Sun & Mon
PRICE RANGE: $$$$
NEIGHBORHOOD: Centro

Upscale Michelin eatery offering a menu of classic Italian cuisine. They have 5 or 7 course tasting menus available. The service is exquisite to the point of being tiresome. Very elegant, however. If you fall asleep, they'll give you a gentle nudge. I tried once ordering the 5-course tasting menu, but it took just as long as the 7-course endurance test. Expect dishes like Squab Civet; Mutton tartare (I love this); Risotto with lemon and gentian root; Buffalo Mozzarella (so delicious); Jerusalem artichoke; Southern Italian Stuffed pasta. Assortment of local wines.

NIGHTLIFE

Just a couple of spots I like.

IL GOCCETTO
14 Via de Banchi Vecchi, Rome, +39 06 686 4268
www.ilgoccetto.com/en
Popular wine bar – a locals' hangout. Excellent choice of regional wines, salumi and cheeses. They also sell craft Italian beer and Prosecco. Here you can buy a bottle to go.

JERRY THOMAS SPEAKEASY
Vicolo Cellini 30, Rome, +39 370 1146287
www.thejerrythomasproject.it
NEIGHBORHOOD: Centro Storico
Very cool bar and known as one of the best in Rome.
Only open Wed-Sat, and they stay open late, till 4.
Make a reservation if you want a table (they will give
you a special password to use). Bartenders are pro
and the cocktails are top notch, so try a couple of
different mixed drinks you haven't had in a long time.
Here, they will be made perfectly. If this is your first
time you'll be charged a 5-euro membership fee.

SHOPPING

GELATERIA DEI GRACCHI

272 Via dei Gracchi, Rome, +39 06 321 6668

www.gelateriadeigracchi.it

Popular gelato shop. Flavors change daily and they sell out fast. What makes this place stand apart from other similar shops is its emphasis on different ingredients. **Note: pay** first and take your receipt to the counter to order.

GIOLITTI

40 Via Uffici del Vicario, Rome, +39 06 6991243
www.giolitti.it
This gelato shop (in business for over a century)
offers a large variety of flavors. Near the Parthenon.
Also available is a nice selection of baked goods,
candies, and coffees.

FATAMORGANA

9 Via Lago di Lesina, Rome, +39 06 8639 1589
www.gelateriafatamorgana.com/web/
Here the gelato is smooth, creamy, and light. Nice
selection of unique flavors like ginger hazelnut and
one called "thought" that is actually grapefruit. Or try
the celery-lime or the pimento-chocolate. They sound
terrible, but they taste great.

IL GELATO DI CLAUDIO TORCÉ
Viale Aventino, 59, Rome, +39 06 574 6876
www.claudiotorce.it/
Near the Spanish Steps is this great quality gelato
shop with a great selection of flavors. They offer 20
varieties of just chocolate. (They have about 100
other flavors.)

PASTICCERIA CINQUE LUNE
89 Corso del Rinascimento, Rome, +39 06 6880 1005
www.claudiotorce.it/
Bakery offering a nice selection of pastries, cakes,
biscuits, chocolates, and cookies. There's a pastry
with figs with bay leaf on top that I adore. It's a tiny
space with no name on the door, so be careful, you
might miss it.

PASTICCERIA LINARI
9 Via Nicola Zabaglia, Rome, +39 06 5782358
www.pasticcerialinari.com
A locals' joint, so if you don't follow the rules you may wait a long time. Pay first and take your receipt to the counter. Great pastries, coffees, lattes, and espresso.

INDEX

9 798201 904517